Kings Don't Carry Money

C. Barsotti

DODD, MEAD & COMPANY
New York

1   2   3   4   5   6   7   8   9   10

Library of Congress Catalog Card Number: 81-67420
ISBN: 0-396-08020-0

Of the 140 drawings in this book, 116 appeared originally in
The New Yorker and were copyrighted © in the years 1969 through
1981, inclusive, by the New Yorker Magazine, Inc.

For Ramoth

"*The meeting will come to order.*"

"*Monsieur, may I suggest . . .*"

KINGS
DON'T CARRY
MONEY.

"Wornal, take this plant out and kill it."

"*I'm trained, yes, but not highly trained.*"

"If I were King, I'd eat out."

"*Here, without further ado . . .*"

"*You one of those walking catfish or something?*"

"I have an enormous I.Q."

"Have the fish. Fish is brain food."

"*Now the boys and I would like to sing you a little number.*"

"*So you've read my books and you've brought wine. Good.*"

A REALIZATION

HOME OFFICE
PAY ATTENTION TO THE GUY FROM OHIO. HE'S ON THE SCENE AND HE KNOWS WHAT HE'S TALKING ABOUT.
I'D THROW THAT BIRD OUT OF HERE, BUT HE'S BEEN RIGHT TOO MANY TIMES BEFORE.
CBarsotti

"*I wonder, sir, if you would indulge me in a rather unusual request?*"

"Surprise!"

"'What is art,' Harry? Why do you
ask? You're an accountant."

"Would you like to hear some music while you hold?"

"*Trouble, J. B. Everyone in Accounting is molting.*"

"That's on the house, because you're such a jolly good fellow."

"*Oh! Your husband really is a clown.*"

THE ROLODEX MYSTERIES

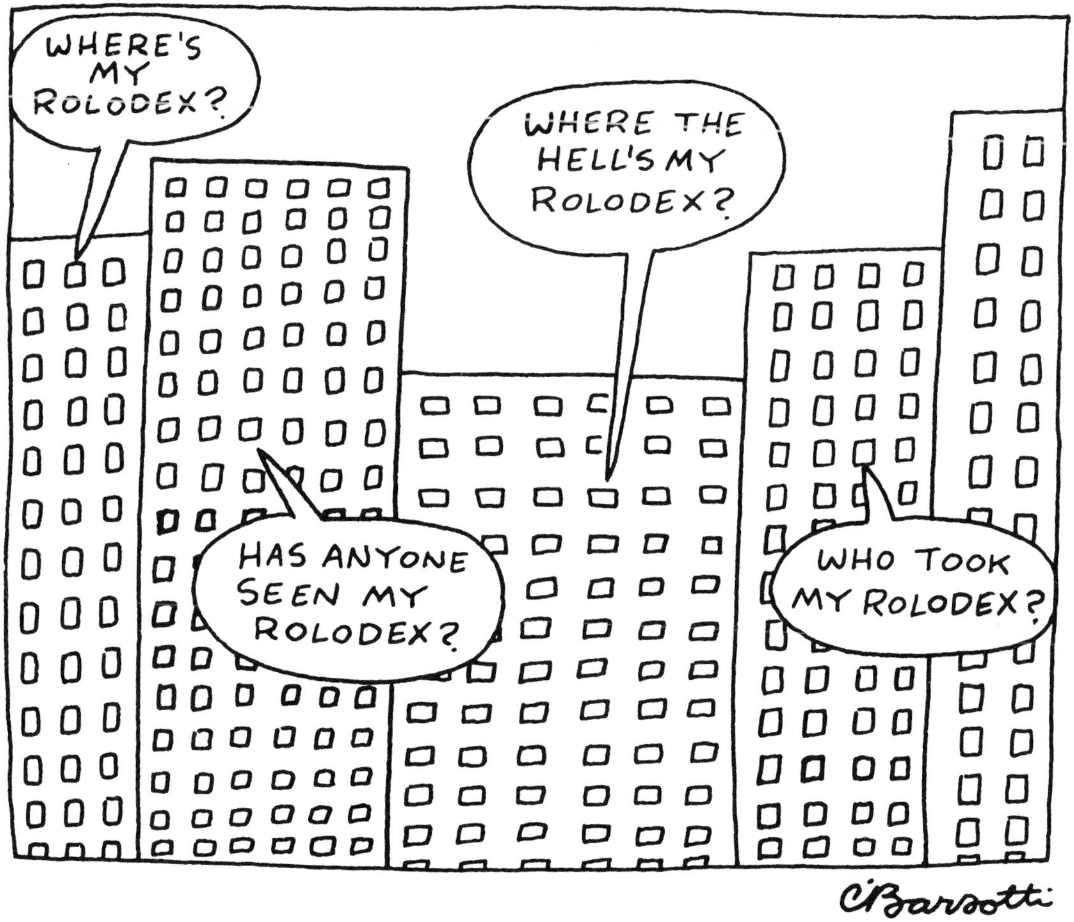

"*Charles, I've had it with you and your goddam moods.*"

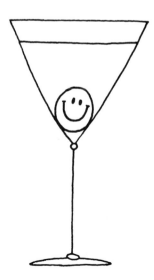

"*Oh, the stories I could tell.*"

"*I work hard and I play hard.*"

VIVE L

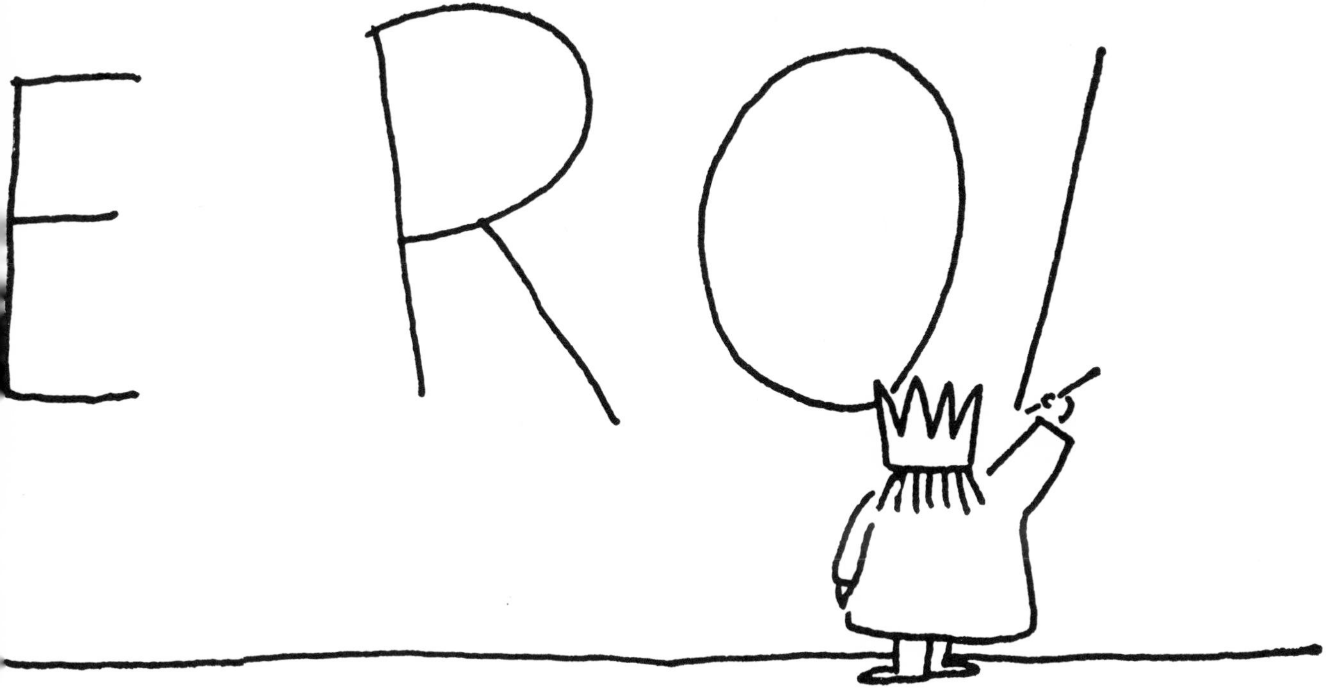
E ROI

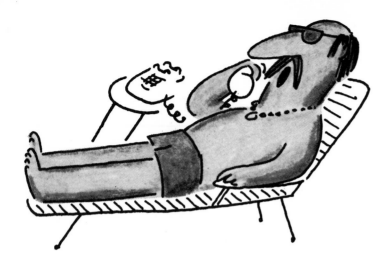

"I'm talking blockbuster, Al. I don't know any other language."

"I'm a king. I don't need dance lessons, thank you."

"*And now for my next number . . .*"

"I blame government, labor, business, and my ex-wife."

"Hi, kid! Did you watch 'Sesame Street' today?"

"'Viable'—that's the word I was looking for!"

"*I'm afraid you'll have to be a little more specific, Ma'am.*"

"*Alice! Alice! I'm out of my funk!*"

"I understand you've learned some new tricks since you were here last."

"Feel better, dear?"

HOW TO GET AHEAD

"Nothing for me, thanks. I'm a hand puppet."

"*Miss Howell, send in the clowns.*"

"*No, wait, Dr. Powers. I have chips to go with the dip.*"

"Yes! Yes! Yes!"

"I answer the phone 'Dickerson here' because
I'm Dickerson and I'm here. Now what the
hell do you want, Martha?"

HOW TO BE A BETTER PERSON

"You took a full-page ad in the 'Times' just to tell everyone that you're <u>confused</u>?"

"*This is your desk. Keep it nice.*"

"Well, hello, what do we have here?"

"Why, it's a book entitled 'How to Be Your Own Best Friend.'"

"I hardly think that we need spend four-ninety-five on that."

"A wise economy. How about a drink to celebrate it?"

"Indeed, sir, a most welcome suggestion."

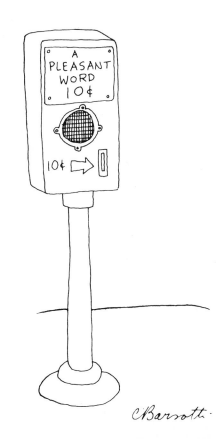

A
PLEASANT
WORD
10¢

10¢

"Keep talking, I'm listening."

"Sure it's a damned inconvenience now. But when
it's published this bar will be famous."

"Thank you for calling Extension 356."

"*Miss Harwood, please see that the halls are decked.*"

"But, Father, is running away ever an answer?"

"Miss Fletcher, send in a pickle."

"Pretty good, but I'll bet you
can't hit him again."

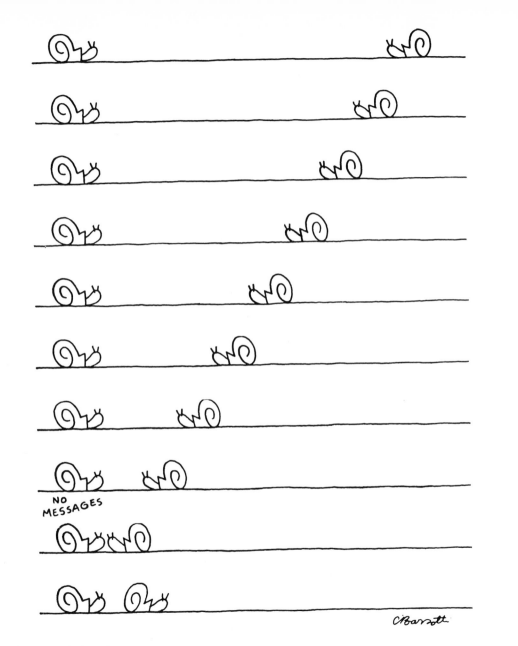

"*For too long, I have been guilty of the crime of silence.*"

"*Twisting paper clips. How about you, Ed?*"

"*Attention all department heads: From now on, we're just going to make small, reliable cars.*"

"You take silver bullets?"

"*He can't come to the phone now. He's indulging the license
society affords those it deems creative.*"

FREE-LANCE TREND SPOTTER

"Ogden, you're not centered!"

cBarsotti

"'Hold,' young lady, is for other people."

"*And what will your little friend have?*"

"I'd like to place a person-to-person call, operator,
to—oh, just anybody."

"I consider myself a passionate man, but, of course, a lawyer first."

"It is we."

THE NIGHT THE SPIRIT WENT OUT OF THE GUYS AT KELLY'S BAR-AND-GRILL.

"*If we got a convection oven the air would go 'round and 'round.*"

PERHAPS I SHOULD PUT ON A DISGUISE AND WALK AMONG MY PEOPLE AND LEARN WHAT THEY REALLY THINK.
ON SECOND THOUGHT, THE HELL WITH IT.
CBarsotti

"*Culpepper, if you don't quit shouting 'Yippee-ti-ay-yea'*
I'm not going to introduce you to the new school marm."

"*I know it sounds exciting, but you're not a wildebeest, and that's that.*"

WHILE YOU WERE AWAY

"*We're the Duderstadt brothers. I believe we have a table for four.*"

"And here's to you, my good right arm."

"Irv Pittman, poolside."

"The old man doesn't want to be called the old man anymore."

"*My first husband wrote five thousand words a day, every day, rain or shine.*"

"*You mean to tell me it does all __that__ for only $14.95?*"

"Adventure's my game."

"I liked him better as a frog."

"No. We _can't_ agree to disagree."

"I'm an economist, ha-ha-ha-ha."

"*That concludes our broadcast day. Go to bed!*"

"*There! There she is! Now go back to the agency and write something for <u>her</u>!*"

"*Yes, Perkins, what is it?*"

AMITYVILLE

CBarsotti

"It's been grand, Mary Lou, but a man's got
to do what a man's got to do, and I've
got to rope goats."

"It makes you look, well, somehow
more thoughtful."

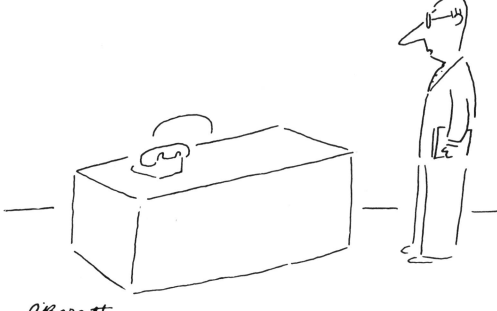

"What's this, Jenkins? Are you absent today or something?"

"*All the interesting traits have been bred out of me.*"

"Shhh. Albert's drawing a rabbit."